Tough Topics

Illness

Patricia J. Murphy

Heinemann
LIBRARY

www.heinemann.co.uk/library

Visit our website to find out more information about Heinemann Library books.

To order:
- ☎ Phone 44 (0) 1865 888066
- ▤ Send a fax to 44 (0)1865 314091
- 💻 Visit the Heinemann Library Bookshop at www.heinemann.co.uk/library to browse our catalogue and order online.

First published in Great Britain by Heinemann Library, Halley Court, Jordan Hill, Oxford OX2 8EJ, part of Pearson Education. Heinemann Library is a registered trademark of Pearson Education Ltd.

© Pearson Education Ltd 2008
First published in paperback in 2009
The moral right of the proprietor has been asserted.

Editorial: Charlotte Guillain
Design: Richard Parker and Q2A Solutions
Picture Research: Erica Martin
Production: Duncan Gilbert

Originated by Chroma Graphics (Overseas) Pte. Ltd
Printed and bound in China by South China Printing Company

ISBN 978 0 431 90785 7 (hardback)
12 11 10 09 08
10 9 8 7 6 5 4 3 2 1

ISBN 978 0 431 90790 1 (paperback)
13 12 11 10 09
10 9 8 7 6 5 4 3 2 1

British Library Cataloguing in Publication Data
Murphy, Patricia J.,
Illness - (Tough topics)
1. Sick - Family relationships - Juvenile literature
2. Separation (Psychology) - Juvenile literature
155.9'3

A full catalogue record for this book is available from the British Library.

Acknowledgements
The author and publisher are grateful to the following for permission to reproduce copyright material:
© Alamy p. 5 (ImageState); © Corbis pp. 4 (Zefa/Grace), 18 (Zefa/Nation Wong), 17 (Reuters), 29 (David P. Hall); © Getty Images pp. 13 (Photodisc), 15 (Stone/Zigy Kaluzny), 20 (Stone/Angela Wyant), 22 (Taxi/Kevin Laubacher), 24 (Stephen St. John); © istock pp. 8 (Eugene Bochkarev), 9 (Peter Elvidge); © Photoedit p. 10 (Bill Aron); © Photolibrary pp. 21 (Corbis), 23 (Bsip), 25 (Image Source Limited), 26 (Photodisc), 28 (Digital Vision); © Punchstock pp. 16, 19 (UpperCut Images), 11; © Rex Features p. 27 (Burger/Phanie); © Science Photo Library pp. 6 (Michaud/Grapes), 7 (James Cavallini), 12 (Adam Gault), 14 (Neil Borden)

Cover photograph of vase of tulips reproduced with permission of © Masterfile.com.

Every effort has been made to contact copyright holders of any material reproduced in this book. Any omissions will be rectified in subsequent printings if notice is given to the publishers.

Disclaimer
All the Internet addresses (URLs) given in this book were valid at the time of going to press. However, due to the dynamic nature of the Internet, some addresses may have changed, or sites may have changed or ceased to exist since publication. While the author and publishers regret any inconvenience this may cause readers, no responsibility for any such changes can be accepted by either the author or publishers.

Contents

Some words are shown in bold, **like this**. You can find out what they mean by looking in the Glossary.

What is an illness?

Everyone gets ill sometimes. Some illnesses, such as coughs and colds, can last a short time and go away by themselves. Other illnesses may last a long time, such as diabetes or cancer, and need special care. These are called long-term illnesses.

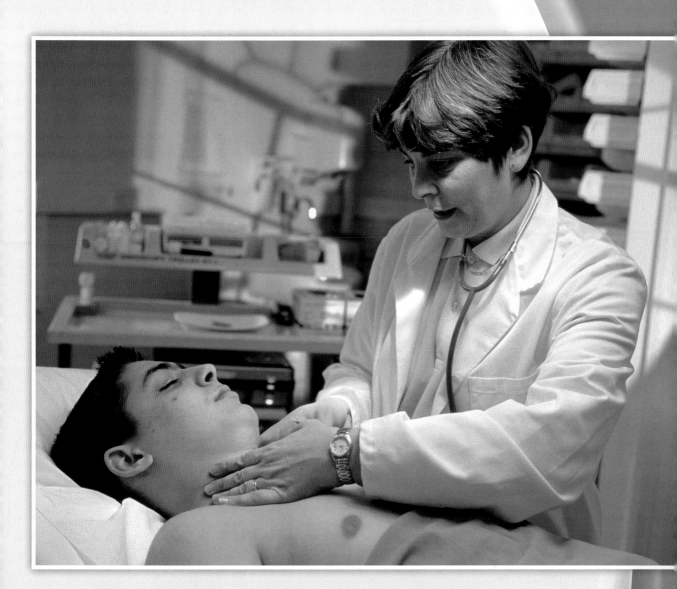

People with long-term illnesses may have to take medicine each day. They may need to receive **treatments** at a doctor's surgery or hospital to get better.

Contagious illnesses

◄ Tiny germs travel in the air and can land on objects when we cough or sneeze.

A contagious illness is a sickness that people can catch from each other. **Viruses** such as colds and the flu spread easily from person to person. Coughing, sneezing, and touching doorknobs or handles are a few ways that people pick up virus germ **cells**.

Doctors can often **prescribe** medicines to clear up some of these illnesses, such as **conjunctivitis**. Many contagious illnesses, such as colds and the flu, must go away by themselves.

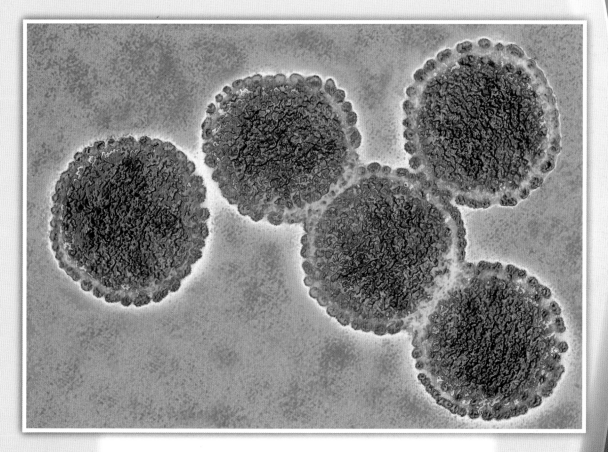

▲This is what a flu virus looks like under a microscope.

Non-contagious illnesses

Many illnesses are not contagious. People cannot catch these illnesses from someone else. People may be born with an illness or develop it later in life. These illnesses include **diabetes**, heart disease, and cancer.

▼ People with diabetes need to check how much sugar is in their blood.

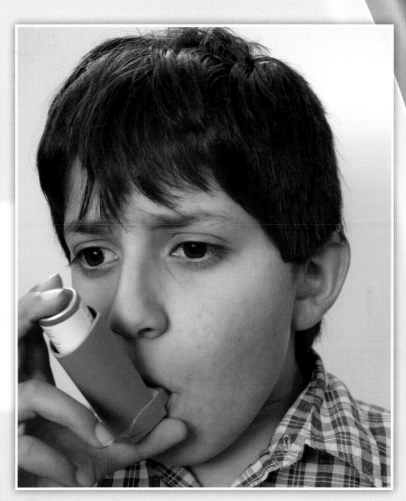

►**Asthma** is a non-contagious illness.

Doctors do not always know why people get certain illnesses. Some illnesses may be **inherited**. Families may pass down the illness from generation to generation.

Long-term illnesses

▲Some illnesses mean that people have to use a wheelchair.

Some illnesses may last months, years, or a person's lifetime. They are called long-term illnesses.

To control these illnesses, people may have to take medicines or receive treatments throughout their lives. They might also have to make changes, such as eating a special diet or getting more exercise each day.

◄ Some people must take medicine everyday.

Common long-term illnesses

◄ This doctor is checking his patient's blood pressure.

Some long-term illnesses include heart disease, **diabetes**, and **asthma**. Most days, people with these illnesses may feel healthy. However, they must see their doctor regularly to control these illnesses.

A person with heart disease may have to take medicine, eat low-fat foods, and get plenty of exercise. Patients living with diabetes may have to check their **blood sugar** levels several times a day and take **insulin** injections to control their illness. People with asthma may take medicines through an **inhaler** to help them breathe.

◄ Everyone needs exercise to stay healthy.

Cancer

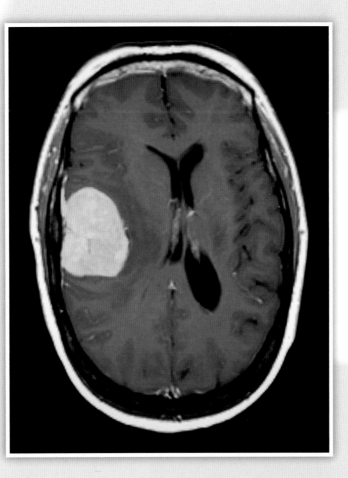

◄ This scan shows a person's brain. The yellow area is a tumour.

Cancer is a common long-term illness. Many types of cancer cause **tumours** to grow in the body. Tumours can harm parts of the body and stop them from working. Some **treatments** can break down tumours.

Some medicines can stop a tumour's growth. Doctors can also remove tumours through **surgery**. Today scientists are working to find new treatments to help control and **cure** cancers.

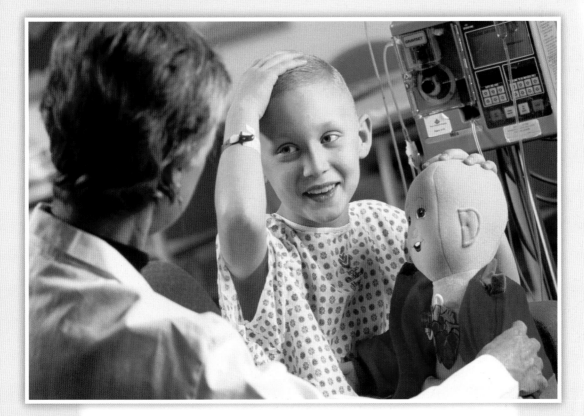

▲This boy has leukemia. It is a type of cancer that affects the blood.

Nerve and brain diseases

Some illnesses can make it hard for people to move. They include multiple sclerosis (MS) and Parkinson's disease (PD). Multiple sclerosis is an illness that affects the nerves and brain.

◄ People living with MS may have trouble walking and keeping their balance.

◄ Michael J. Fox is an actor who has Parkinson's disease.

Parkinson's disease kills **cells** in the part of the brain that controls movement. People living with PD may also have problems moving and balancing, and body tremors or shakes.

Diagnosis

Some people with long-term illnesses may not know they have them at first. Other times, people might have **symptoms** or warning signs of an illness. They may experience a pain, notice a lump, or feel tired or weak.

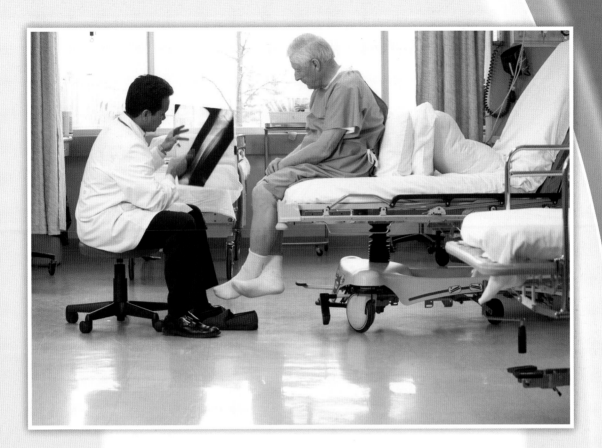

▲ This doctor is showing his patient
an X-ray picture.

Doctors may order special **X-rays**
or tests to see what is wrong. Once
doctors have the X-ray pictures or test
results, they can make a **diagnosis** and
choose the best **treatment**.

Treatment

Today there are many different ways to treat illnesses. These **treatments** may help control the effects of an illness or cure it. Many people with illnesses must take special medicines every day.

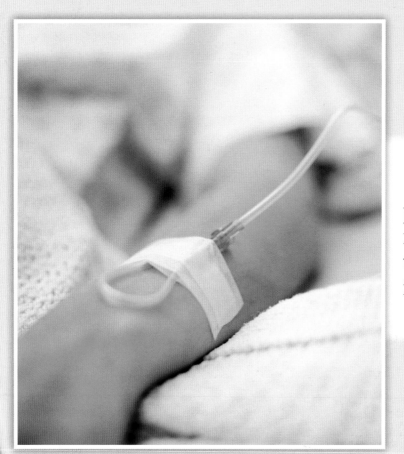

◄Some people receive medicine through veins in their arms.

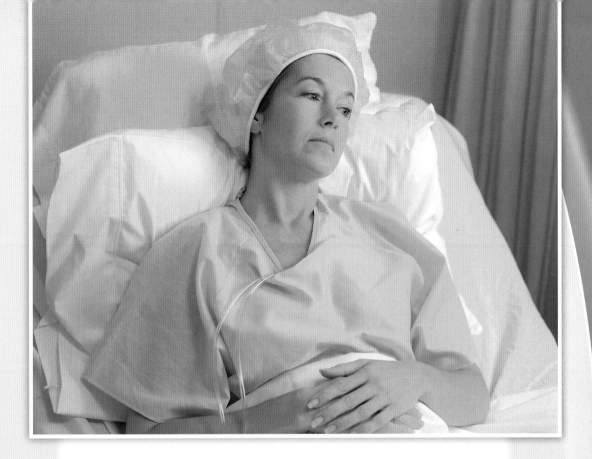

▲ This woman is waiting to have surgery.

Some people must stay in a hospital to receive treatment. They may need an operation or other special care. Sometimes these people cannot have visitors because they may be very sick or catch germs easily.

Side effects

◄ This patient is having chemotherapy to treat cancer.

Whenever people take medicine for an illness, there may be **side effects**. These happen when a medicine that helps one part of the body hurts another part. For example, **chemotherapy** that helps kill cancer **cells** also kills hair cells. That is why many people lose their hair while they are going through chemotherapy.

There may also be problems after having **surgery**. People may have to rest for a few weeks or months to let their bodies heal. If they need to be in bed a long time, they may also need help to strengthen their legs and arms.

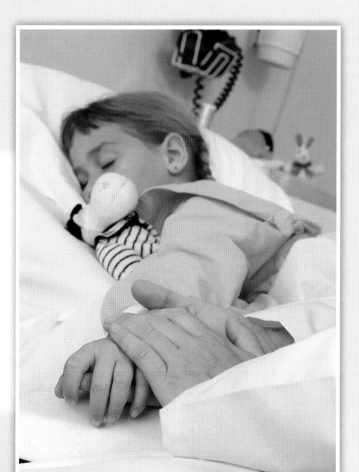

▶People can be very tired or weak after surgery and may feel some pain.

Coping with a loved one's illness

When someone you love is ill, you may have many different feelings. You may feel sad or angry because you do not want your loved one to be ill. You may worry that you might get ill, too.

◄ You may wonder why your loved one is sick and think that it is unfair.

◄ Tell your loved one what you are worried about.

You may also worry that your loved one will not get better. It is okay to have these feelings. They show that you love and care for your loved one very much.

Getting help

▲ Talk to your friends and family about your feelings.

It is a difficult time when someone you love is ill. Sometimes, you may be filled with all kinds of feelings. Other times, you may not know what to feel or do.

You could try talking to your loved one or send cards and letters. You could also talk to someone you trust, such as a family member, friend, or teacher to share your feelings.

▲ You can share your feelings with a **counsellor** or doctor.

Living with illness

In many cases, people will get better and feel healthy again. They are able to do the same things as before and return to a normal life. Other times, they may live with an illness and continue taking medicine or getting **treatment**.

▲Many people can have a happy and active life after illness.

▲Having an illness in your family can bring you all closer together.

After a loved one's illness, you might feel that you have grown and learned things because of the shared experience. Going through this may help you realize that there are many ways to treat and live with illness.

Glossary

asthma disease that makes it difficult to breathe and causes people to cough or wheeze

blood sugar amount of sugar in your blood. It gives the body energy.

cell smallest part of a living thing

chemotherapy medicine that is used to treat cancer

conjuncitivitis eye disease

cure make someone healthy

diagnosis doctor's decision about what is causing someone to feel ill

diabetes disease caused by too much sugar in the blood

disease long-term illness

inhaler tool that allows people to breathe medicine into their lungs so they can breathe more easily. People with asthma use inhalers.

inherit when something is passed down from your parents

insulin something in the body that helps control the sugar in the blood so the body can work normally

leukemia cancer of the blood

prescribe order for use as a medical treatment

side effect unwanted reaction to a drug

surgery operating on a patient

symptom sign that shows you have an illness

treatment way in which medical care is given

tumour mass of cells in the body caused by illness

virus tiny organism or life form that makes people sick

X-ray high beam of light that can pass through solid objects and take pictures of teeth, bones, and other organs in the body

More books to read

Asthma (It's Not Catching), Angela Royston (Heinemann Library, 2005)

Flu (It's Catching), Elizabeth Laskey (Heinemann Library, 2002)

What Does it Mean to Have Diabetes? Louise Spilsbury (Heinemann Library, 2002)

What Does it Mean to Have Epilepsy? Louise Spilsbury (Heinemann Library, 2003)

I Feel Sick! Mick Manning and Brita Granstrom (Franklin Watts, 2003)

Do I Have to Go to Hospital? A First Look at Going to Hospital, Lesley Harker and Pat Thomas (Hodder Children's Books, 2006)

Index